realU
GUIDE TO
YOUR FIRST APARTMENT

MEGAN STINE

GUIDE TO YOUR FIRST APARTMENT
TABLE OF CONTENTS

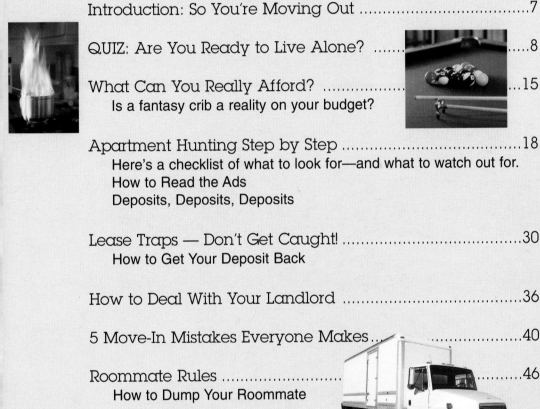

YOUR FIRST APARTMENT

So you're moving out...

School? Been there, done that.

Hanging around your parent's house? You're over it.

That rent-free apartment over your aunt's garage, with the windows painted shut and the broken air conditioner? Don't even ask.

Maybe you're leaving home for the first time, heading off to college... Or maybe you're skipping the college thing and sliding straight into a real job and real life... Or maybe you've left home before, come back, left, come back, left—so many times that your parents are starting to wrap your birthday presents in road maps. (As in "Happy Birthday to our 30-year-old. Now, get out!") Whatever.

This guide will tell you all you need to know to move out of the house, find an apartment, and start your life for real.

So turn the page, get ready to have one of the best adventures of your life, and start checking out the cold hard facts about moving into your first crib.

And welcome to

real U

ARE YOU READY

Getting out of the house or dorm may sound like the best thing since soap-on-a-rope. But are you really ready to take the rap when your rent check bounces? Or cope when the toilet backs up into the tub? Can you even be *trusted* with an oven mitt?

TAKE THIS QUIZ AND FIND OUT!

1.

Let's say you're still living at home, but your parents have blown out of town on a vacation to Maui. It's 10 o'clock at night and you're starving. You open the fridge to face a vast cavernous nothingness. We're talking ketchup, maybe a spoonful of dried mac & cheese stuck to the inside of a baking dish. What are you going to do? You:

A. Pick up the phone, call your best friend, and whine until he offers to bring you a hot sub and a six-pack.

B. Drink the ketchup, lick the dried cheese out of the casserole, and call it dinner.

C. Head for the grocery store to shop like it's Armageddon, stocking up on enough food to feed the whole family when they return.

TO LIVE ALONE?

2.

Straight out of school, BAM—you land a job. You graduate on Sunday, start work on Monday, sign a lease on Tuesday, move into your new apartment on Wednesday. (Okay, so you're lucky.) On Thursday, your two closest friends decide to hit the highway for a major road trip, and they want you to come along. You:

A. Pack your bags and kiss that first job goodbye. Easy come, easy go, right? Besides, you figure you can probably land another job the day after you get back.

B. Call in sick on Thursday, Friday, and half of next week so you can hang for at least part of the road trip. And cross your fingers that you'll still be employed when you get back.

C. Tell your friends, "Sorry, I just signed a lease. Send me some postcards." Then sit home watching E!'s *Wild On* and planning a monster vacation for later this year.

road trip!

more quiz ⟶

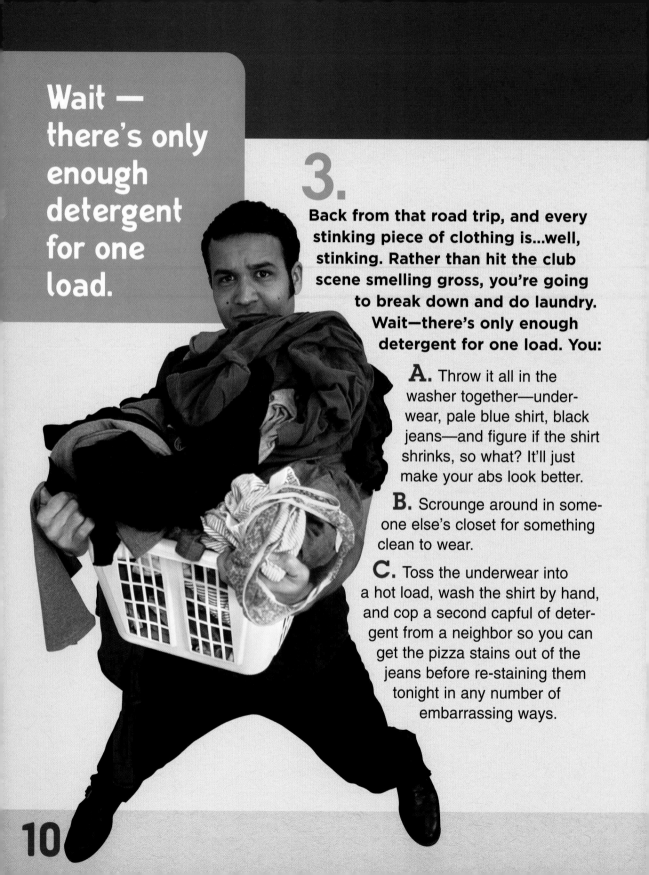

Wait — there's only enough detergent for one load.

3.

Back from that road trip, and every stinking piece of clothing is...well, stinking. Rather than hit the club scene smelling gross, you're going to break down and do laundry. Wait—there's only enough detergent for one load. You:

A. Throw it all in the washer together—underwear, pale blue shirt, black jeans—and figure if the shirt shrinks, so what? It'll just make your abs look better.

B. Scrounge around in someone else's closet for something clean to wear.

C. Toss the underwear into a hot load, wash the shirt by hand, and cop a second capful of detergent from a neighbor so you can get the pizza stains out of the jeans before re-staining them tonight in any number of embarrassing ways.

4.

You're two weeks into a new relationship and you're trying to seal the deal by cooking something amazing for your love bug. You've got olive oil heating in a sauté pan, you're chopping onions and green peppers, and...hey! the kitchen's on fire! Or at least that pan of olive oil is a blazing inferno. You:

THE KITCHEN'S ON FIRE!

A. Scream, panic, and toss water on the thing, causing hot oil to splatter all over you and scarring you for life. (Effectively ending your chances with the love bug, by the way.)

B. Try to remember—is it "drop and roll" or "rock and roll"?

C. Calmly toss a lid on it to suffocate the flames—even you know oil and water don't mix, especially when fire's involved.

more quiz ⟶

Are you really ready to take the rap when your rent check bounces?

5.

The longest period of time you've ever spent entirely alone is:

A. Two hours in 1999 stuck in an elevator.

B. All of third grade.

C. Let's just say you maxed the score for "Forest Ranger" on that Meyers-Briggs aptitude test you took in high school.

SCORING

Face it—people who turn magazines upside down to learn something about themselves are generally unprepared to live on their own. But there may be hope for you yet—if you can figure out how to turn this thing right-side up and plow through the rest of the guide. Okay, okay, calm down, don't whine. You want a score? Fine. The right answers are C.

Give yourself one point for each right answer.

SCORE OF 4-5:
You're obviously so competent that you probably should have moved out long ago. You've got a sweet deal going there, letting your parents pick up the slack. We won't tell if you don't.

SCORE OF 3:
You're clearly the type of person who can figure out how long to nuke a piece of frozen pizza without calling home. On the other hand, you still sort of like it when your mom makes you a grilled cheese sandwich. In other words, you're ready to tackle living on your own, but you might want to keep your best friend on speed dial for the first few months.

SCORE OF 1-2:
One word: roommates. Seriously consider having some other warm bodies in the place when you move into your first apartment. Like maybe ten of them. But hey—that sounds like fun! And besides, no one said you have to take the plunge into real life all at once. With a little support from family and friends, you should be fine.

you gotta start somewhere...

14

WHAT CAN YOU REALLY AFFORD?

We all know what you want. But when it comes to renting your first apartment and starting life on your own, you've got to face the realities.

Admit it. If you had your choice, you'd move into one of those fantasy cribs filled with cool leather furniture, pool tables, hot tubs, a wet-bar in every bedroom, uber-chic walk-in closets, and seven gorgeous roommates who…

Hang on. That's an MTV reality show which, as we all know, is anything but real.

In the world the rest of us inhabit, stuff costs money, and you'd be surprised how fast it adds up. So before you sign a lease on your dream apartment, whip out your calculator and find out what it really costs to live on your own. To give you a rough idea about the ka-ching involved,

we've invented two technically bogus but 100% reality-based typical average 20-something singles.

So turn the page and check out Josh and Madison, their stories and their lifestyles. Then use the blank space in the chart to fill in your own expenses and figure out exactly how much "reality" you can afford.

15

JOSH & MADISON

JOSH: **Typical hypothetical average everyguy**

Age: 22

Roommate: Ben, high-school best buddy/ slacker/leech

Backstory: Just graduated with BA in Broadcast Journalism

Job: Clerk in video store

Salary: $10 per hr. = $1,505/month

Take-home Pay: $1,053 per month

Budget Breakers: Clubbing on Saturday night, monthly gym membership

MADISON: **Typical hypothetical average everygirl**

Age: 23

Roommates: Yellow lab and 3 cats

Backstory: Moved away from home two years ago after bailing out of cosmetology school

Job: Waiting tables at Siesta Corners

Salary: $2 per hr. plus tips = $1,935/month

Take-home Pay: $1,354 per month

Budget Breakers: Cashmere sweaters, eating out with friends

	JOSH	MADISON	YOU?
Rent	$375/mo. Josh's half of $750	$680/mo.	
Gas Electric	$20 $22 Josh's half	Included with rent	
Phone	$39.95 cell phone plan	$29.95 cell, $24 land line	
Internet	$15	$0 Still using her parents' account	
Cable TV	$18.50 Josh's half	$48 w/ movie package	
Groceries	$430	$300 She gets 1 free meal/day at work	
Transportation	$0 He bikes everywhere.	$150 car insurance $40 gas. Her parents paid for the car. Sweet!	
Laundry/Dry Cleaning	$28 Three loads of wash/wk, and that wool coat of his hasn't been cleaned in 6 months.	$56 More silk, more sweaters, and she wants to keep them looking good.	
Entertainment	$60 That's $15/wk. for movies and club- bing. He gets his DVD rentals free.	$120 More dinners out, more movie rentals, and she hangs out drinking lattes at Internet cafes.	
Medical/Dental	$0 Teeth cleaning? What's that?	$0 Parents are still covering her.	
TOTAL EXPENSES	$1,008.45	$1,447.95	
INCOME / SALARY	$10 per hr. = $1505/ Month	$2 per hr. plus tips averages $90/night $1935/Month	
TAKE-HOME PAY After taxes & withholding	$1,053.00	$1,354.00	
WHAT'S LEFT OVER? For clothing, savings, holiday gifts, vacations, and emergency fund!	$44.55	$0 NOTHING! She's over-spending every month, running up her credit card bill.	

17

APARTMENT

YOU'VE GOT TO SETTLE ON PRICE, LOCATION, AND AMENITIES. THEN, UNLESS YOU HAVE UNLIMITED CASH, PICK TWO.

HUNTING
STEP BY STEP

Finding the right apartment is always a juggling act. You've got to start by asking yourself three questions. What can you afford? Where do you want to live? And what features do you need in your new apartment? In other words, you've got to settle on price, location, and amenities. Then, unless you have unlimited cash, pick two.

Why only two? Because that's how it works. If you find an apartment for the price and in the location you want, you won't get all the amenities—no balcony or extra bedroom, for instance. Or you can get all the extra features—maybe two bedrooms and a balcony, in a new building with off-street parking—but if it's affordable, it probably won't be in a prime location. Or you can get the great location and all the cool features, but the price is going to bust your budget. In short, you have to decide what's important to you, and where you're willing to compromise.

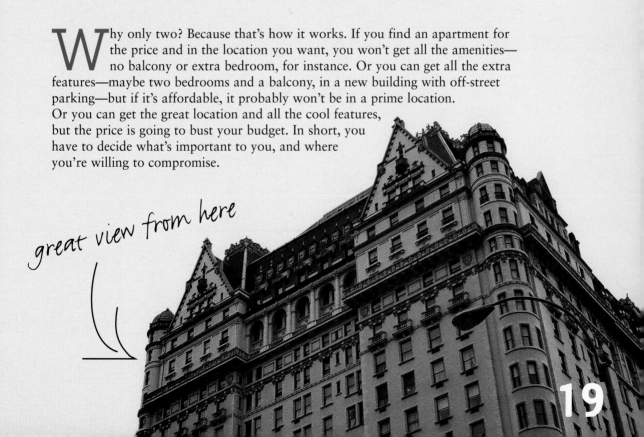

great view from here

19

6 STEPS TO FINDING YOUR FIRST APARTMENT

STEP ONE

Decide how much you can afford.

The chart on Page 17 will help you keep it real when you're figuring out how much to spend on rent each month. Don't forget to include the cost of phone, utilities, and cable TV.

STEP TWO

Scope out the choices and decide where you'd really like to live.

Do you want to be close to friends and family, work or school? Is it important to be able to walk to movies and shopping? Or are you a nature lover who craves peace, quiet, and a few green trees outside your window? What about transportation? How close is the Post Office? Ultimately, your choice will be dictated in part by budget, but you've also got to find a neighborhood and location that fit your lifestyle.

STEP THREE

Start reading the classified ads in the newspaper,

or pick up one of those apartment rental magazines which are available free in the grocery store. (They're often stacked up in a rack near the entrance.) You can also find Internet listings for apartment rentals in larger cities. The ads should give you a good idea about the price range for each neighborhood. See Page 22 for help decoding all the terms you'll encounter in the classifieds.

STEP FOUR

Hit the streets and start looking at apartments.

You may be surprised to find out how the real thing stacks up to the description in the ads. Shop around so you'll know what's out there in your price range, and try not to take the first apartment you see. However, the best apartments are often snapped up fast, so have your checkbook ready in case you really love the place.

STEP FIVE

Ask questions!

What's included with the rent? Utilities? A free parking space? How about cable? What are the rules about pets? Can you paint if you hate the colors? What are the late payment fees if you don't pay the rent on time? Are you allowed to sublet the apartment? Read the lease and ask more questions.

STEP SIX

Apply for the apartment.

Believe it or not, apartment hunting is a little like job hunting. You've got to dress for the part and present yourself well or the landlord may not choose to rent to you. Of course it's illegal for landlords to discriminate on the basis of age, sex, race, national origin, or religion. But they do have the right to ask about your income and run a credit check. They can also turn you down if they suspect you're going to trash the place or keep the neighbors awake with some off-the-wall habits, so leave your bagpipes at home.

WHAT DO YOU MEAN "NO CABLE"?

Believe it or not, some older buildings aren't wired for cable. If television is important to you, ask before you move in.

Be prepared to pay an application fee, which is usually not refundable. Landlords will also often ask for a number of references—including a reference from your previous landlord. Since this is your first apartment, you can't score points this way. Instead, try to make a good impression by showing up with your resumé and a copy of your credit report in hand. If you don't have a resumé, be ready to give a few extra references from your boss, old family friends, or even old high school teachers. If you're not sure how to get a copy of your credit report, visit www.realuguides.com.

Lastly, read the lease again, ask more questions, and then—only when you're sure you understand everything—sign it. See Page 31 for lease traps to avoid.

HOW TO
READ THE ADS

You don't have to be a **CIA** code-breaker to understand the abbreviations and terms used in the classified ads. All you need is this quick glossary of terms

STUDIO:

An apartment with just one room for living and sleeping. Sometimes there's a separate kitchen, sometimes only a small "kitchenette" opening into the main room.

JUNIOR ONE BEDROOM:

Otherwise known as "Honey, I Shrunk the Bedroom." This is a one bedroom apartment where the bedroom is really small and not necessarily a separate room—just an alcove off the main living space.

LOFT:

Usually a large, open apartment in a building formerly used as a warehouse. Lofts often have exposed brick walls and an open floor plan.

TOWNHOUSE:

Much like a house, a townhouse has an upstairs, a downstairs, and its own separate outside entrance, but it is attached to other similar units.

CONDO:

Any apartment which is owned by an individual rather than rented from a landlord. When you buy a condo, you actually own the walls and floors of the building—and you are responsible to maintain them. Sometimes a condo owner will rent out his apartment to a tenant.

A fourth-floor walk-up can be killer when you're hauling a bike or a duffel full of laundry.

what were we thinking?

CO-OP:

Similar to a condo, except that co-op owners don't actually own the walls and floors of their apartments. Instead, they co-operatively own shares in the building.

BROWNSTONE:

An older, narrow three- or four-story building in a city, usually made of stone or brick. Brownstone buildings were private homes when they were built, but many have now been converted to apartments.

WALK-UP:

That's what an apartment in a brownstone is called—especially if it's on the top floor. A fourth-floor walk-up can be killer when you're hauling a bike or a bag full of laundry.

FLAT:

In England, this is what they call an apartment.

3BR/1.5BA:

BR means bedroom, BA means bath. When an ad says 1.5BA, it means there's a full bath (with shower or tub) and a half bath with only a sink and toilet.

ABBREVIATIONS:

EIK: Eat-in-kitchen

RIV/VU: River view

F/P: Fireplace

DW: Dishwasher

W/D: Washer/Dryer

A/C: Air conditioning

UTIL. INCL.: Utilities are included with the rent. Excellent!

23

12 THINGS TO LOOK FOR IN AN APARTMENT

Some features are frills, some are necessities. Here's a list of what to look for and what to watch out for when shopping for an apartment.

this closet is too small!!

1 SAFETY

This isn't a frill; that's why it's number one on the list. Make sure the building you're moving into has enough security features for the neighborhood it's located in. Is the front door to the building locked at all times? Are the windows secure or could a burglar easily climb in from the street? Is there a peephole in the door so you can see who's knocking? Is the exterior lighting bright enough so you can see if someone's lurking outside when you come home at night? Are there adequate smoke detectors? Check out the safety features and consider the safety of the neighborhood as well.

2 PARKING

Is there off-street parking for your car, or will you be hunting for a space every night after work? (Or every day after class.) If you don't have a car, is public transportation nearby?

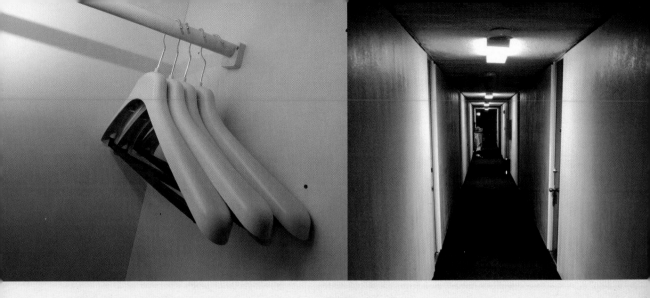

3 NOISE

Apartment noise comes in two forms: annoying sounds from outside the building, and annoying sounds from the neighbors. In buildings with thin walls and floors, you'll hear your upstairs neighbors clomping around day and night, so you might be happier with a place on the top floor. Traffic noise is the other problem, so when you're apartment hunting, open the windows and ask yourself: if I open them in nice weather, will the street sounds drive me crazy?

4 ACCESS

You may not think you'll mind climbing stairs to a third-floor walkup apartment, but it can get old when you're lugging your bike or three bags of groceries every day. Seriously consider a building with an elevator.

5 CLOSETS

Check to make sure you'll have enough room, not just for your clothes but for things like skis, bikes, vacuum cleaners, winter coats, towels, extra bedding, your life-sized cardboard cutout of Elvis, and anything else that might become a storage headache.

6 FLOOR SPACE

Rooms look larger when they're empty. Remember that your furniture can fill up the space pretty fast.

7 WALL SPACE

It's not just for posters! Remember that even if the rooms are large, you can still wind up with no wall space for furniture, thanks to windows, closet doors, radiators, and archways.

good water pressure

8 APPLIANCES & PLUMBING

Try the stove, try the faucets, flush the toilet, and check the water pressure and hot water. Test the air conditioner, even if it's winter when you're considering this apartment. (And by the way—does the place even have an air conditioner?) Same goes for testing the heat in summer. Make sure everything's in working order when you first see the apartment. If it isn't, that may be a sign that the landlord spends more time worrying about his golf game than he does about repairs and maintenance.

Small kitchens can become an issue if your roommate is a vegan who buys ten-pound bags of brown rice at a time.

9 KITCHEN STORAGE

You probably don't own six sets of dishes, twenty-four wine glasses, or a deluxe set of pots and pans, so kitchen cabinet storage probably isn't a problem. Yet. But some kitchenettes are so tiny, there's barely room for a toaster oven on the counter top. A small kitchen can become an issue if your roommate is a vegan who buys 10-lb. bags of brown rice at a time.

$625 a month!

10 ELECTRICAL OUTLETS

Newer buildings will have plenty of electrical outlets but older buildings might not. If you own enough electronic devices to stock your own media store, you may not be happy—or safe, for that matter—in an apartment with insufficient outlets.

11 DAYLIGHT

Don't go apartment hunting at night. You won't have any idea whether the rooms are dark, dingy, and cavelike, or sunny and well-kept.

12 LAUNDRY ROOM

Basically, is there one in the building? If not, you'll have to lug your clothes to a laundromat every week. Good for meeting people, not necessarily great when you need a clean pair of socks on short notice.

RENTER'S INSURANCE: PLAY IT SAFE

Picture it. You've been in your apartment a few months and you come home one night to find the door ajar and your laptop gone.

This is a nightmare no matter how you slice it since you'll have to replace all those e-mail addresses and personal files, to say nothing of the work you may have lost at the same time.

But the loss is even worse if you have to shell out your own cash to buy a new computer. That's why renter's insurance is an excellent idea. For about $300 a year, depending on where you live, you can buy a renter's policy which will protect your property from theft, fire, and other losses. Renter's insurance also protects you when the worst kinds of accidents happen—for instance when you leave a frying pan on the stove and set the whole building on fire. Seriously consider a renter's policy. If you can't afford it, maybe you can talk your parents into footing the bill.

laptop and jewelry – gone!

DEPOSITS DEPOSITS DEPOSITS

Before you move out of your parents' house, you'll need to save up a chunk of change for these one-time, upfront costs.

DEPOSIT ON APARTMENT

In many parts of the country, you'll have to put down a security deposit when you sign a lease. The deposit protects the landlord in case you stiff him on the rent, or do some kind of damage—your cat ruins the rug, for instance, or you break the light fixtures.

How much is the deposit? It can be as much as a full month's rent, or in large cities, even more. Or it may be as little as $50. And you won't get it back until you move out, leaving the apartment in the same condition you found it on moving day. (See Lease Traps on Page 31 for more about getting your deposit back.) Just remember that the deposit is in addition to the first month's rent which you'll also have to pay in advance.

DEPOSIT ON UTILITIES

When you call the gas and electric companies to have service turned on in your name, you may be asked to pay a deposit. The utility companies hold this money as insurance, in case you skip town without paying your bill. You'll either get it back when you move out, or the money will be applied to your final bill.

Sometimes, if you already have a good credit rating, your deposit may be smaller—or you may not have to pay one at all. But you might have to pay another kind of fee—a service charge— to have your accounts set up or to have the service turned on. Again, if your credit rating is decent, they may not ask for the service charge up front, but be prepared to pay it when your first monthly bill arrives.

DEPOSITS ON PHONE AND CABLE TV

Ditto. Everything we said about the gas and electric company can be true for phone service and cable. Again, it depends on your credit rating and what part of the country you live in.

LEASE TRAPS

- No overnight guests allowed.
- No music after 10:00 p.m.
- 50% late fee for overdue rent.

Don't Get Caught

If you're a first-time apartment renter, you may look like fresh meat to a landlord when it comes time to sign a lease. So don't reach for your pen too soon.

A lease is a legal contract. It obligates you to pay the rent each month for the term of the lease, even if you move out, in many cases! It also explains who is responsible for maintenance or damage and sets down the rules you have to follow while you're living in the apartment. If your lease says "no pets," for instance, you can't adopt a cute little floppy-eared fuzzball, no matter how adorable it is. Break that rule and you could be evicted—legally forced to move.

Always read the lease carefully, and ask questions before you sign.

Here's a look at some of the specific points you'll want to think carefully about.

the lease says no pets!

TERM OF THE LEASE:

How long are you going to live in this place? Face facts: if this is your first apartment, you really don't know whether you're going to like living alone—or how well it's going to work out with that crazy roommate you've hooked up with. For first-timers, a short-term lease can be ideal, if the landlord will agree. Depending on the area of the country you're renting in, you might be able to talk the landlord into a six-month lease—which could be good for you, if you want to bolt after six months. It could be bad, however, if you live in a highly desirable area and the apartment rents go up fairly fast. In that case, you might want a longer lease to protect you from rising costs.

SUBLET CLAUSE:

Subletting is the term for renting your apartment to someone else. If you need to move out for some reason—to accept a job in another city, let's say, or simply because you've got a sudden urge to explore the South American rain forests—you may want to sublet your apartment. Before you sign, check the lease to see if subletting is permitted. If not, you could be stuck paying the rent for the whole term of the lease.

LEASE CANCELLATION:

Does the lease spell out terms for cancellation? Sometimes you're allowed to break your lease with 30 days written notice, but there may be a cash penalty involved. If possible, add a sentence to your lease which will allow you to move out if your circumstances change.

YOU OR YOUR ROOMMATE: WHO SIGNS?

In most cases, you and your roommate will both need to sign the lease in order to protect your rights to legally share the apartment. In some cases, you might be allowed to sign the lease yourself and then take in a roommate at a later time (especially if you have a sublet clause). But don't kid yourself—if your name is the only one on the lease, then you're the only person legally responsible to the landlord.

Having two names on the lease doesn't really let you off the hook, because in that case, you and your roomie are both 100% responsible for the rent. In other words, if your roommate gets fired or skips town, you don't get to claim that you only owe your half of the rent. You signed, so you owe the whole thing. Of course so does she—but if she's long gone or out of work, whom do you think they're going to come after? You—the person who still has money in the bank.

LATE FEES:

How much can the landlord charge you if you fail to pay the rent on time?

AUTOMATIC RENEWAL:

Many leases will automatically renew at the end of the term unless you tell the landlord in writing that you plan to move out.

SECURITY DEPOSIT:

See Page 35 for more about this. The key point here is that you want to be sure the lease spells out exactly what's required for you to get your deposit back.

PAINTING POLICY:

Does it say you're not allowed to paint the walls? Did the landlord or his managing agent wink and say, "Oh, it's okay, as long as you don't paint the place black." Don't fall for it. You could wind up in trouble if the landlord tells you one thing verbally and then puts a different policy in the lease.

UTILITIES INCLUDED:

If the landlord says that water and garbage service are included with the rent, make sure it's in writing. The same goes for other utilities or cable service.

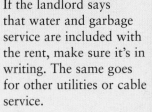

NO LEASE

You may live in a part of the country where landlords are so eager for tenants that they're willing to rent month-to-month, with no lease. Great! you figure. You can move anytime, right? Yes, but the downside is that the landlord can kick you out at any time, too, with only 30 days notice in most cases.

ROOMMATES AND OVERNIGHT GUESTS:

Some leases have a clause limiting the number of people who can live in the apartment, and some even say you may not have overnight guests. If you think you might want to add a roommate, plan ahead.

Their lease says roommates okay!

LANDLORD'S ACCESS:

By law, the landlord must be able to get into your apartment at reasonable hours to make repairs or show the apartment to new tenants when you're ready to move out. You have the right to privacy, however, and to be given reasonable notice about visits from the landlord. To find out more about your rights, visit www.realuguides.com.

PETS:

No fuzzy creatures allowed unless the lease says so. Not including your brother, of course.

HOW TO GET YOUR DEPOSIT BACK

1. **Before you sign your lease, make sure you've inspected the apartment carefully and noted any existing damage.**

   Then put it in writing, in the lease, and have the landlord initial it.

2. **Ask for a move-in inspection.**

   Walk through the apartment with the landlord after the old tenant moves out, and before you move in. You may notice more damage, now that the other guy's stuff has been removed. Put it in writing.

3. **Photograph the whole apartment before you move in, to document the condition.**

   Color prints are fine, or use a camcorder. Use a camera with a date stamp. Or, if you want to be extra-careful (some people might call it "paranoid") place a current daily newspaper in the photographs to identify the date. If you take the pictures during the walk-through inspection with the landlord, he'll know you're serious about getting your deposit back.

Broken before I moved in!

4. **Photograph the place again when you leave.**

   Take the same pictures, from the same angles.

5. **Clean the apartment well when you move out.**

   Not only will it look better when the landlord comes to inspect, but it says, "I'm not the kind of person who would leave the place a mess." You're more likely to get your deposit back if the landlord knows that a) you know your rights; b) you're responsible; and c) you take the situation seriously.

If you don't get your deposit back, you can sue the landlord in small claims court. You'll need proof, however. Now aren't you glad you took those photographs?

WHEN SOMETHING

Trouble from the landlord is usually some form of: it's broken and he doesn't want to fix it.

GOES WRONG ...
HOW TO DEAL WITH YOUR LANDLORD

There are two kinds of problems you can have with your landlord—trouble that's your fault and trouble that's his or hers.

Trouble from you is usually some form of: you can't pay the rent. If this happens to you it can lead to eviction, which is a serious problem. See more about eviction on Page 39.

Trouble from the landlord is usually some form of: it's broken and he doesn't want to fix it. Maybe the faucet is leaking, maybe you have critters under the kitchen sink, maybe there's never enough heat at night or hot water in the morning. Whatever the problem, the best way to deal with the landlord is to follow the four basic rules on the next page.

the stove never works!

it's always freezing in here!

1.
Put everything in writing.

Sure, you may want to start by phoning the landlord (or the managing agent or superintendent of your building). Ask for the problem to be fixed. But if it doesn't happen quickly, follow up with a polite letter stating the problem. Date the letter, keep a copy for yourself, and mail it with a return receipt requested.

2.
Get everything in writing.

If your landlord promises to buy you a new stove, ask him to e-mail you with a specific date when you can expect it to be installed. If he or she offers to put in new carpeting as a perk to get you to renew your lease, get it in writing.

3.
Know your rights.

You have a right to a clean, safe, sanitary and habitable living space, with adequate heat, hot water, and electricity. If your apartment has serious problems, you may have the right to have the problems repaired, and then deduct the cost from your next month's rent. In some cases, you may have the right to move out without being obligated for the remainder of the lease. For more information on tenant's rights, visit www.realuguides.com.

4.
Be polite.

You'll have more success if you don't go ballistic, either on the phone or in your letters to the landlord.

EVICTION

worst day of my life!

Y ou can be evicted for non-payment of the rent, or for any number of other serious violations of the terms of your lease. As a practical matter, though, most landlords won't bother evicting you for the minor stuff—an occasional noisy party, for instance—unless they have another reason for wanting you out. (A classic example: They want to raise the rent and evicting you is the only way around your long-term lease.)

If for some reason you can't pay your rent on time, the best thing you can possibly do is pick up the phone, call the landlord, and fess up. Tell him or her what your special problem is— maybe you just lost your job, or had an expensive medical emergency. Make a partial payment if possible, and give an honest estimate of when you'll be able to pay the rest. In other words, communicate. It may not keep the landlord from evicting you, but it's the best shot you have at buying a little time and staying in your home.

If for some reason you can't pay your rent on time, the best thing you can possibly do is pick up the phone, call the landlord, and fess up.

5 MOVE-IN

It's harder to find an available rental truck at the end of the month, so reserve in advance or you might not find one.

MISTAKES EVERYONE MAKES

Moving Day can be the most fun you've ever had without snack foods—especially if you manage to avoid these five classic mistakes.

1

NO ELECTRICITY

Why is it so hot in here? And dark? When the rental agent showed you the apartment, the lights were on, the A/C was working, and you just assumed it would always be thus. Right? Now it's moving day and you're sweating like crazy as you haul boxes and furniture in from the street.

The problem is: you've made a classic mistake. You've forgotten to have the utilities turned on in your name. Meanwhile, the previous tenant wised up and realized she

was paying for electricity she's no longer using. She called the utility company and closed her account. (Or, if she was a little slow on the draw, the power may not go off for a few more days. Right in the middle of your first party, for instance.)

To avoid this particular disaster, make sure you've set up the utilities in your name before you move in.

Don't forget to have the electricity put in your name!

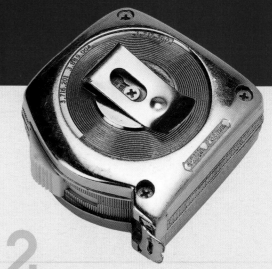

2
SIZE
MATTERS

Before you accept a hand-me-down sofa from your great uncle, remember that size matters and ask yourself: Will it fit? There are so many ways you can have trouble trying to get a couch or other long piece of furniture into a small space. And that goes double if you're moving into an old building with narrow stairs or small elevators.

So scope out the situation with a tape measure before you move in. Then make sure you invite a sufficiently large number of friends and relatives to help with the heavy unwieldy stuff.

3
AVOID
COMIC RELIEF

There's no nice way to say this, so let's just cut to the chase. Bring toilet paper to the apartment before you start moving in. It wouldn't hurt to kick in a bar of soap and a hand towel, too. Your friends will thank you.

4
AVOID THE 30TH

So you've packed the truck and sweet-talked four buddies into helping you move. You pull up in front of the apartment building and...hang on. You don't pull up in front of the apartment building. In fact, you can't even get near the place because there are three other moving trucks already parked outside. What's going on? How come so many other people came up with the same brilliant plan to move in on the same weekend as you?

Most people move at the end of the month, right around the thirtieth. Or they pick the weekend closest to that date, which can mean you'll be competing with several other people for parking spots, elevator usage, or the stairs in your new building. It's also harder to find an available rental truck at the end of the month, so reserve in advance or you might not find one.

One way around this scenario is to move in a few days after your lease starts— like, say, on the fourth or fifth of the month. Or on a Wednesday. The traffic will be lighter, and it's less embarrassing. As in, your new neighbors will be at work, so no one will witness you struggling to get that life-sized cutout of Elvis/Ringo/Britney up the stairs.

5
LABEL THE ESSENTIALS

Once the stuff is in the apartment, chances are you're too whipped to unpack it all right that minute. You just want to shower, snack, and snooze. Or better yet, go out and party like... well, like you just got a new apartment. Uh-oh. Where are your hot rollers? Your toothbrush? Your razor?

The easy fix for this move-in mistake is label everything. Mark the boxes with the kitchen stuff so you can eat breakfast in the morning. Mark the iron, so you can show up looking decent for work or class. Mark the alarm clock so you'll be on time for work. Better yet, pack all the essentials in one box and just label it Open Me First.

KITCHEN

Before You Move In...

don't forget the phone!

- ☐ Turn on utilities in your name
- ☐ Turn on phone service
- ☐ Turn on cable TV
- ☐ Reserve rental truck
- ☐ Mail change-of-address forms
- ☐ Shop for basic household products

- ☐ Stock apartment for moving day: cold sodas, paper cups, toilet paper, soap, paper towels, box cutter
- ☐ Measure doorways and stairs for large pieces of furniture

BONUS TIP!
HOW TO AVOID 16 TRIPS TO THE SUPERMARKET

Frankly, this tip is a scam because it's almost impossible to avoid 16 trips to the supermarket. You'll go out for a broom and forget to buy a dustpan. Go out for light bulbs and forget to buy an extension cord. But here's a list of basic things you're likely to need when you move into a new apartment. No promises, though—we probably forgot something, too.

- ☐ box cutter
- ☐ broom
- ☐ dust pan and dust mop
- ☐ sponges
- ☐ cleaning products
- ☐ dish and laundry detergents
- ☐ paper towels and holder
- ☐ screw driver
- ☐ hammer and nails
- ☐ picture hangers
- ☐ duct tape
- ☐ soap and shampoo
- ☐ toilet paper and tissues
- ☐ wastebaskets

- ☐ trash bags
- ☐ light bulbs
- ☐ extension cord
- ☐ plunger
- ☐ bucket
- ☐ fire extinguisher (It'll make your parents happy.)
- ☐ The Clapper® (It'll make your friends happy.)

we need another bathroom!

46

Roommate Rules

Most people can handle the small stuff— dirty dishes in the sink or a forgotten phone message. The trouble usually starts when you've missed a tenth phone message...or the dishes are never clean. Or when there are major issues, like money. If someone can't pay his share of the rent, it's going to be a serious problem for everyone.

The best way to make sure that you and your roommate won't end up hating each other—or at least minimize the likelihood — is to choose the right person from the beginning. The trick here is to avoid kidding yourself, because often your best friend will make the worst roommate.

Sure, you and your best friend can hang at the mall for six hours without getting on each other's nerves. That's why you've been friends since second grade. But is he a world class slob while you're a closet clean freak? Does he like 70's disco and you're addicted to indie rock? Does he like to drag home every warm body he can find and plop them down in front of ESPN for hours and hours—while you'd rather watch movies, and you'd

kill for a few minutes of privacy? Does he party all night while you'd prefer to hit the sack at 11:00? Ask yourself the hard questions before you decide to live with someone. If it turns out that your best friend isn't prime roommate material, it's better to admit that fact now— before you ruin a great relationship.

There's no way to guarantee you and your roommate will always get along. But you have a fighting chance if you work out the rules and regs in advance. Some roommates even go so far as to put it in writing—a roomie "pre-nup" of sorts. They split up the chores, make a cleaning schedule, and list all the do's and don'ts. Then they put it up on the fridge, so everyone knows what he or she is expected to do. Whether you spell it all out in a contract or just have a

47

thanks for cleaning up!

heart to heart talk, it's best to face these questions before you sign a lease together.

Once you've picked a roommate, it's time to consider the financial deal. What happens if he loses his job and can't pay his share of the rent? How long will you be able to carry the load yourself? Also, work out who's going to pay the bills. Maybe you'll take turns paying the cable bill every other month, or maybe you'll split it down the middle each time. Maybe you want to put the phone in your name and the electricity in his name. Make sure it's fair, and that you both understand and agree. And

remember that anything in your name is your responsibility if your roommate can't or won't pay his share.

When you're ready to start sharing a microwave with someone, sit down first and ask yourself which of the following situations are deal breakers? Then you'll have a better idea about your own personal bottom line.

SITUATION	DEAL BREAKER	NOT A DEAL BREAKER
You end up doing all the cooking.		
Your roommate never cleans up after meals.		
Your roommate thinks she owns the mayo and wants you to buy your own.		
Your roommate stays up all night and you usually rise at dawn.		
You want your own phone line but your roommate insists on saving money by sharing.		
He/she never writes down your phone messages.		
One TV and she wants control of the remote.		
You're always cleaning the bathroom. And it always needs it.		
Your roommate borrows your favorite sweater for a hot date or a job interview.		
Your roommate borrows your favorite sweater every other day.		
You've put a sock on the doorknob— your signal for "Do Not Disturb." Your roommate barges in anyway.		
You've agreed to write the rent check each month. Your roommate never pays his half on time.		
It's a no-smoking house, but your roomie lets his friends smoke.		
Your roomie takes up much more than his half of the space.		
You call a meeting to discuss it when the above rules fail, and your roommate never shows.		

49

HOW TO
DUMP YOUR
ROOMMATE

If you've tried to work things out
and failed, it might be time to move on.
Here are some tips about handling it.

IF THE LEASE IS IN
YOUR NAME
ALONE:

Have a heart to heart with your roomie and tell her you want her to move out. Calmly tell her why. Don't try to place any blame—it's probably as much your fault as hers. (And if not, you can score big points by saying so anyway.) Give her a decent amount of time to find someplace else to live. And remember that it can be fairly traumatic to be thrown out of your home, so give your roommate plenty of time to move—even if you have her replacement waiting in the wings.

IF THE LEASE IS IN
BOTH NAMES:

Your roommate has as much right to the apartment as you do. So have a talk with her and explain that you'd like to make a change. If she's willing to move and you can afford the rent alone, great. Otherwise, you'll have to be the one who leaves. But be careful: your name is on the lease, which means you're still legally responsible for the rent. Offer to help her find a new roommate. Then have a talk with the landlord and ask that a new lease be drawn up without your name on it.

Don't try to place any blame—
it's probably as much your fault as hers.

51

All About

RULE NUMBER ONE FOR FRESHMEN:
call your new roommates as soon as you find
out their names and make a plan in advance.

Dorm Rooms

Life in a dorm can be one big endless party... or an ongoing nightmare of cramped space and no privacy... or something in between.

So how do you make sure that your first home away from home is as comfortable and familiar as the room you've left behind? Check out this list of the best ways to make your dorm room cozy, cool, and, if you're lucky, a super magnet for the opposite sex.

1. LIGHTEN UP.

Which in this case means bring lamps—as many as you can jam into the back of your parent's mini-van (after you've loaded your other stuff, of course). Nothing makes a dorm room more pleasant or appealing than good lighting, which you'll never get from those awful fluorescent overheads. Consider bringing not only a nice big table lamp for your desk, but also a floor lamp to stick in the corner of your room. If you're flying to school and shipping your stuff, you can hit a discount store when you get to college and buy the lamps there.

I got a single this year!

53

Nothing makes a dorm room more pleasant or appealing than good lighting, which you'll never get from those awful fluorescent overheads.

2. FLOOR SHOW.

A rug, even an inexpensive one, will make your dorm room seem more like home, feel good on your bare feet on cold winter mornings, and serve double duty when 15 friends drop in at the same time (and you only brought 14 chairs from home).

3. THE TV, THE MINI-FRIDGE, THE BONGO DRUMS: WHO BRINGS WHAT?

Rule Number One for freshmen: call your new roommates as soon as you find out their names and make a plan in advance. (This assumes your college is smart/kind/enlightened enough to send roomie contact info before orientation.) Otherwise, you'll end up with three televisions, four refrigerators and, quite possibly, not enough bongo drums. It's a disaster you'll be glad to avoid.

CREATIVE COLLEGE HOUSING

Considering the cost of college housing, which can average $5,254 per year at state schools and $6,455 at private colleges and universities, many families are coming up with a money-saving alternative plan. Parents are choosing to buy a house near campus which their son or daughter can live in for their sophomore, junior, and senior years. (Freshmen usually live in dorms.) The cost of the mortgage each month is covered by renting out several rooms in the house to other college students who are friends or former roommates. At graduation, the house can be worth more than the parents originally paid, making it a good investment. Even if the house doesn't appreciate in value, the savings in college housing costs can be impressive.

REAL STORY

Deric's family bought a house in Amherst, Massachusetts in 1999 for $99,000. The house needed some TLC, so Deric and his friends painted the place throughout and fixed it up. The mortgage payment was $1,000 each month. Deric rented rooms to three friends for $400 each, for a total of $1,200 per month. When he graduated in 2001, his parents sold the house for $129,000. Bottom line, Deric's college housing at the University of Massachusetts was free for two years, and his family made $30,000.

Is your lava lamp really worth the price of boxing it up and shipping it there?

Kitchen

DISHES

FRAGILE

56

MOVING *WAY OUT*

LIFE IN ANOTHER CITY

It's one thing to move into an apartment a few miles from home. It's a much bigger deal to move to another city or state halfway across the country. Here are a few of the special circumstances you'll face.

GETTING THERE

If you're making a long-distance move, you might be tempted to rent a truck or hire a mover to haul your stuff to the new location. Before you plunge into this, however, do some math. Is your lava lamp really worth the price of boxing it up and shipping it there? The cost of hiring a professional mover can exceed the value of your furniture and possessions. And renting a truck can be expensive—not to

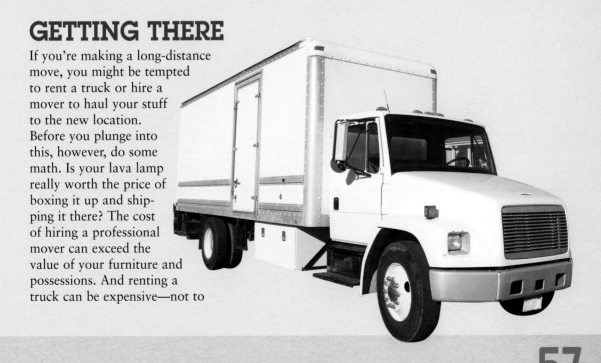

In larger cities like **New York,** the best apartments are frequently not advertised in the newspaper—they're only listed with rental agencies.

mention the fact that the minimum age for renting vehicles is usually twenty-five. It may be cheaper to simply take whatever you can stuff into your car, and buy everything else when you reach your destination.

If you do decide to hire a mover, be very careful. There are dozens of ways to get burned by professional movers. Learn more about hiring a mover at www.realuguides.com.

APARTMENT LOCATION SERVICES

In some cities, you may need the help of an apartment real estate agent or broker. This is because in larger cities like New York, the best apartments are frequently not advertised in the newspaper—they're only listed with rental agencies. But don't assume that you're always in good hands with a rental agency. Depending on the city, it may be typical and reasonable for you to pay a fee to the agency—or it may be completely unnecessary and even a rip-off. How so? Some "rental agencies" are actually paid by various apartment complexes to steer you to their properties. The bottom line is: you need to find out what's customary in the city you're moving to. Try to talk to someone locally—a family friend or a relative living in the area—who can give you advice.

RENTS AROUND THE COUNTRY

Take a look at the typical rents for one-bedroom apartments in cities around the U.S. Figures are accurate as of 2004.

$3800 in New York!

Denver, CO	$625
Miami, FL	$770
San Francisco, CA	$800
Milwaukee, WI	$530
Columbus, OH	$395
New York City, NY	$2000
Boston, MA	$775
New Haven, CT	$609
Madison, WI	$635
Atlanta, GA	$650
San Diego, CA	$720
Dallas, TX	$622
Chicago, IL	$925
Seattle, WA	$595
Nashville, TN	$425

This lamp is perfect!

FURNISH IT FOR UNDER $300

It's not hard to furnish your new apartment on a shoestring budget. All it takes is a little begging and borrowing, a few cans of paint, and a trip to the Salvation Army.

Let's start with the begging and borrowing, which basically amounts to asking your parents and other relatives for hand-me-down pieces of furniture. You can probably score a bed this way—especially if your parents are eager to get rid of you. With luck, you might also come up with a dresser from your aunt, a lamp from a neighbor, or an end table that your grand-mother forgot she had in the attic.

Then it's on to the flea markets, the Salvie, and the Goodwill shops. Whatever you can't borrow from fam-ily, you can probably buy on the cheap. An ugly $15 dresser will look amazing with a fresh coat of paint and some new knobs. You might also find an old thrift shop sofa. Don't worry about how grungy it looks in the store. You can buy a ready-made cotton duck slipcover for about $129 and no one will know what's underneath.

What else is essential? A coffee table is major for the living room. But try to find

Throw pillows can double as seating on the floor.

great flea market finds!

a camp trunk, wicker basket, or antique wooden box which can double as storage space. Then put an air mattress inside so you'll always have room for overnight guests. And if you must buy a bed or a sofa, go for the 2-in-1 deal and get a futon. You can sit on it by day, fold it out for sleeping at night.

Remember, the key to making your apartment look fabulous is to put your money into a few special items—some great throw pillows, for instance, or a wonderful lamp. The throw pillows can double as seating on the floor. And the lamp will become the focal point of the whole room if you put it somewhere special—on a low table, for instance—where everyone will notice.

Last but not least, don't forget to put some art-work on the walls. One great trick is to make black-and-white copies of your favorite photos. (Use a color copier for best results.) Blow them up, frame them in identical frames, and call it a gallery. Who's going to argue?